THE WONDERFUL WORLD OF CATS

THE
WONDERFUL
WORLD OF
CATS

Julia Freeman

CONTENTS

Acknowledgments

The publishers would like to thank the following organizations and individuals for their kind permission to reproduce the pictures in this book :

Animal Photography Ltd.: 7, 11 below, 13, 27 above, 29, 35, 37, 39 above, 45 below, 46 below, 47 above, 50 above & below, 51 above, 54 above, 55, 58, 59, 60 below, 64 above, 65, 66 above & below, 68, 69, 81 below, 95 below, 95 right, jacket front above and centre right, jacket back; Auto Trends: 86 below; Barnaby's Picture Library: 33 above, 34 above, 74 below, 79 right, 82, 83, 87 above & below; Bavaria Verlag: 15, 49, 94; Sdeuard Bisserot: 56, 75 above; B.P.C.: 9; Camera Press: 38-39, 41 below, 61, 86 above, 93; Bruce Coleman Ltd.: 71, 77; Anne Cumbers: 2-3, 17, 19 below, 26, 52 below, 70 above, 78 below; C.M. Dixon: 28; Fox Photos: 95 above left; F.P.G. Inc: 53, 54 below, 57 above, 70 below, 75 below, 76 below, 81 below; Will Green: 43 above, 92 above; Sonia Halliday: 42; Michael Holford: 8, 10, 11 above, 12; Louise Hughes: 67; Jacana Agence de Presse: 32 below, 33 below; Keystone Press Agency: 81 left; John Moss: 22, 23; Natural Science Photos: 85 below, 88, 89 above; Octopus Books Ltd.: jacket front left, endpapers, 63, 64 below; Pictor: 1; Pictorial Press: 52 above, 74 above, 79 below; Peter Smith: 76; Spectrum Colour Library: 16, 18, 19 above, 21, 27 below, 30, 31 below, 34 below, 41 above, 44, 45 above, 47 below, 60 above, 85 above, 89 below, 92 above, jacket front above right; Tony Stone Associates Ltd.: 4-5; Syndication International: 31 above, 38 below, 51 below; Betty Whitmore: 73; ZEFA: (Paul Friese) 84, (J. Grossauer) 25, 32 above, (Gerolf Kalt) 46 above, (Gary Clewis) 40, (Mohu) 91, (F. Park) 43 below, 57 below, (G. Thorlicheu) 80 below, (Hed Wiesner) 80 above.

First published 1976 by
Octopus Books Limited
59 Grosvenor Street, London W1

ISBN 0 7064 0563 3

© 1976 Octopus Books Limited

Produced by Mandarin Publishers Limited
22a Westlands Road, Quarry Bay, Hong Kong

Printed in Hong Kong

ENTER THE CAT

It is an interesting fact that the domestic cat is absent from classical mythology. Dogs and horses and birds abound; serpents and bulls, those ancient symbols of strength and fertility, are encountered at every turn; even monsters are invented to explain some half-understood fear. But the cat, the resourceful and graceful creature that could symbolize so much, is no part of our legacy from the ancient cultures.

The explanation is that the domestic cat is a relative newcomer to the company of man, and she is unique as the one and only animal that man took to himself for a non-utilitarian purpose. That she is the supreme enemy of small vermin is really a bonus that man earned by the way. She may well have taken to man because rats and mice were to be found wherever he dwelt – but that is a different story. Her independent nature and capacity for keeping her own counsel make her a very different pet from the slavishly adoring dog, and one can be sure that the cat's acceptance of man is certainly on her own terms.

She joined him about 5,000 years ago, a miniature of the royal symbol of the lion which must be considered before we can understand how the cat walked into man's company and in a short space of time exacted veneration from him. She was a god before she ever became a pet.

The lion has been a symbol of power from the time that man first knew him. The creature was more widely distributed in ancient days; it was as familiar in western Asia as it is in Africa now, and makes an appearance in the ancient traditions of the Hindus. Appropriately, it symbolizes power; sometimes in divine form and sometimes in royal – it would be nearly impossible to draw a division between the two, since kings in early cultures were usually the representatives of gods if not gods themselves. Western Asia and Egypt are regions where the sun can kill as easily as it can give life-stirring warmth, and in ancient times it was feared and propitiated as much as it was invoked. The lion was the creature which symbolized solar heat.

The creature has almost vanished from India just as it has from western Asia, and its survival in Hindu tradition suggests that the migration of peoples which took the Aryans into India must, on the journey, have led them through the same sort of territory that their racial kindred, the Persians, made their home. The Hindu scriptures describe the deeds of the god Vishnu, and ascribe to him various appearances on earth when evil was abroad and man was suffering. One of these occasions saw the assumption of divine authority by a king who demanded that his subjects and his family acknowledge him as a god. One of his sons refused, in spite of deprivation and, eventually, torture. The watchful god decided that it was time to make another appearance on earth – his fourth, according to the scriptures – to destroy the power of the evil king. He came to earth in the form of a lion.

It was in Egypt, lion country in ancient times, that the cat became a god and where she first entered the household. The history of this great empire of antiquity was of such duration that it encompassed a great range of beliefs. It also saw a constant shift of power from one region to another and the syncretization of a fantastic number of local religions to form a faith acceptable to all. With the shift of power there was often a shift in fashionable religion – the ascendancy of Amon, the ram-headed god of Thebes, occurred when that city became the centre of power. An older city, Memphis, was where the lion as the symbol of solar light and brilliance found its chief expression about 5,000 years ago.

The creator god of Memphis was Ptah, represented by the bull; his consort was the lion-headed Sekhmet. Ptah generated life in a cow by his rays and his bull, the moon creature, represented fruition and growth. But the moon gives way to the sun, the ripener, which never waxes or wanes and which in spite of its benefits is to be feared. For this reason Sekhmet was called the Eye of Ra – she personified the sun god's destructive heat.

As we have seen, things were always changing in Egypt and though the sun god Ra endured, he became Amon-Ra when the centre of power moved to Thebes about 3,500 years ago; Amon, the ascendant deity, took to himself the character of his rivals. The sun god still crossed the heavens during the day and still sank into the western horizon at night. He travelled, people said, in the solar barque, and before he could resume his journey over earth from the eastern horizon he had to pass through the dark regions below. His reappearance each morning was greeted with hymns of thankfulness.

One of the dangers faced was the great serpent Apep who waited eternally in the shades, hoping to destroy the sun on its journey, and a later tradition tells how the solar barque carried the Eye of Ra, who fought the serpent nightly, and nightly overcame it. But the Eye of Ra was no longer the fearsome, lion-headed Sekhmet. The Eye of Ra was now a cat. This was change indeed.

What had happened? The answer is quite obvious –

The Black Short-hair (*right*) is considered nowadays to be a lucky omen. But in the Middle Ages the cat was linked with the devil. Hundreds of people were tortured on suspicion of being witches and the cats, who were believed to be their familiars, were tortured and burned with them.

puss had arrived on the scene and had taken over, as she always does.

A familiar creature in the Near East and Egypt was a feline species known as the Caffre cat, an animal a little larger than our house cat. The Caffre was regarded with favour because it preyed on, among other things, snakes and this was important to the people of the marshy region of the Nile Delta. Treated with respect, eventually with affection, she found her way into the temples, those man-made regions of coolness, and it wasn't long before the Egyptians, who made gods of every living creature, bestowed divine honours on the cat. A cult developed; the cat was acknowledged as the goddess Bast and her cult centre became the city called Bubastis. Sekhmet came to be regarded as one of the goddesses of olden times. The cat was cherished in the temples and there, when she died, she was embalmed and buried with full funerary honours. Anyone foolish enough to kill her paid for the crime with his life.

However, everything changes, even for divine cats. They became accustomed to the company of man and eventually entered his house. Condescending to domesticity, they carried with them a suggestion of sanctity and this led to a regard that even the most besotted cat-lover of today might think excessive. When the house cat died in ancient Egypt, the whole household went into mourning; everyone cut off their hair and observed elaborate rites before embarking on the waiting period while another cat made up its mind to take possession of the empty place. To the Egyptians every cat was the same cat, so to speak; the goddess Bast incarnate.

Having arrived, one might expect that the cat would have become a familiar part of the households of the ancient world. But, just as she is missing from Greek mythology, she is missing from the Greek people. We have evidence that she was *there*, and little more than that. And this is curious because the lion, her mighty cousin, was well known to the Greeks. He appears on Cretan seals and there is a celebrated survival, the Lion Gate of Mycenae, which may represent the ascendancy of the sun and sky gods who supplanted the cult of the Earth Mother; but the small cat seems to have meant nothing to them. They kept dogs, and had a charming habit of making cages for crickets and cicadas because they enjoyed their chirruping. There is a reference to a cat in one of Aristophanes' plays, but the context suggests a wild cat, and a creature which *could* be a cat turns up on one or two Greek vases. That is all – no cat, no animal in fact, would ever have be-

The lion goddess Sekhmet (*left*) was revered by the Egyptians 5,000 years ago as the personification of the sun god's destructive heat. But when the cat arrived, a new cult developed; divine honours were bestowed on her and she was acknowledged as the goddess Bast (*right*).

9

come a god for the Greeks.

The Romans were different. It is true that they used small snakes and weasels to kill mice, so the appearance of the cat in Rome probably stems from two facts: they were the lords of Egypt and they were, especially the wealthy patricians, fascinated by novelty. Egyptian cults made a deep impression on them and it was inevitable that the pampered puss of the Egyptian household would find a similar place in Rome. As prolific then as she is now, the cat would soon have outgrown her place in wealthy households and been obliged to make do with the common people. Fifty years after the Battle of Actium the elder Pliny was referring to the cat as a well-known creature to be seen everywhere.

Rome became mistress of the world, as we know. The centuries of her rule bestowed order on a large part of the world and where the Roman went the cat went too. There was another cat in the wild regions – but that one shunned the company of man. She kept company with the goddess Frigga of the Teutons and the wild cat was, and is, virtually untamable. Nevertheless, the wild and domestic strains met and commingled and to this we owe much of the variety in size and colouring displayed by our domestic cats. In Western Europe under the Roman occupation 'The ordinary livestock of a villa included horses, cattle, sheep, and pigs; geese were often kept, and cats and dogs were, of course, in-dispensable' (Collingwood and Myers: *Roman Britain and the English Settlements*).

The statement is fascinating, not least because it is so positive. Unfortunately, the Pax Romana did not endure; in the fifth century AD the Romans abandoned their conquests and departed to try to meet the danger threatening the Eternal City. Western Europe was left to undergo a nightmare of violence and destruction and when some degree of order and civilization returned, it was to a world so crippled in the soul that the lighter, more graceful side of Graeco-Roman culture lay buried until the Renaissance, nine centuries later.

This was to prove hard on the cat. The very qualities that had made her welcome to civilized man – her beauty, her grace, her independent nature, her nocturnal pleasures, her seeking the company of those who made least demands on her and gave her the most comfort in return – were to make her an object of suspicion in a fear-riddled and superstitious society. When once the cat became associated in the minds of people with the idea of witchcraft, the poor creature was to endure unspeakable treatment at the hands of men.

There was another reason for Western man's attitude to the cat in medieval times. Where the torments of hell were promised to anyone who departed from the church's ruling, and where this rule had lately replaced

The Greeks did not bother with small cats but they admired lions, as is seen by the statues on the Terrace of Lions at Delos, the Greek island (*above left*).

A beautiful bronze cat called the Gayer Anderson cat (*top*) from the British Museum.

The Abyssinian cat (*above*) is thought to resemble some of the cats of ancient Egypt. It was here that the cat was a sacred animal and rigorously protected by religious law.

paganism – which was in most of Europe – the memory of the old beliefs was strong. It would not have been long before this time that the people of the northern plains had known the cat as the corn-spirit, and dissuaded their children from molesting the growing corn by telling them that the corn-cat lived there; that in many parts of Gaul the last sheaf of corn was called the cat's tail, and that before the reaping began a cat was garlanded with flowers and ribbons; that in Silesia the reaper who cut the last sheaf was called Tom-cat and given a pointed tail to wear; that in Picardy a cat was offered as a sacrifice when the harvest was gathered in. These were the old beliefs and, said the churchmen, the old beliefs were the devil's work. It must follow that the cat was the devil's creature, and would only consort with those who served him.

The church, anxious and insecure, gave no quarter to those who made the slightest departure from the rules, and for centuries the charge of heresy against a person, or a community, could result in ruthless and bloody persecution. It was an age when charity seemed to have departed completely from the men of God.

It has to be acknowledged that heretical movements were frequent in Europe in the early Middle Ages; centuries were to pass before the power of Rome succeeded in quelling the mere thought of a different belief. The statements made at heresy trials are, at this distance of time, quite staggeringly idiotic; but they were believed, and thousands of men and women died because of them. Again and again there is mention in them of a cat, usually as the devil himself. It was said of the Cathars that they held secret conventicles in which the devil was worshipped in the form of a cat. Gregory IX, the pope who founded the Inquisition, gave instruction to the Archbishop of Mainz to preach against heresy in Germany. The pope knew, apparently, exactly how heretics were initiated – one might wonder *how* he knew. He told the Archbishop that the heretics sat down to a communal meal and, before giving themselves over to abominable lusts, received among themselves a black tom-cat. The novice was fully received only after he had kissed the tom-cat under the tail. The cat turns up in the trials of the Luciferans at Marburg, and in those of the Knights Templars in France.

It went very hard for the cat that she had ever been designated the corn-spirit in the old religion. Her presence – when the heretical movements had been crushed and the Inquisition had time for smaller game – was to bring the scales down against the survival of many people who were isolated, or withdrawn, or simply the victim of someone's spite.

But society then, as now, moved on several levels. The poor had no one to speak for them and the rich did much as they liked and had no hesitation in deciding what was good for others. The first witchcraft

trials took place in Europe in the thirteenth century but there is ample evidence that the kings and nobles, while agreeing that cats and witches must be burned together, did nothing to keep the cats away from their own palaces. The monasteries always kept cats, for the simple reason that the cat was, in spite of the lunatic convictions that overcame the churchmen at witchcraft trials, the main defence of people everywhere against vermin. It might be wondered how a single cat could have survived the madder seasons; but puss is a nimble creature and good at taking care of herself. She survived. When the universal church and the Inquisition had passed from the earth she was still there, ready to sit with man – if she felt like it.

But her reputation for strangeness did not depart quickly. The last trial for witchcraft took place in England in 1712, the last in Scotland in 1722; in both a cat was named as the witch's familiar. Cardinal Wolsey, the most powerful and probably the most hated man in England for fifteen years, took his cat to the dinner table, to audiences and to the cathedral when he was officiating at services. Richelieu, more powerful even than Wolsey, loved cats and gave orders that they be maintained at court. Hated as much as Wolsey, his predilection must have suggested something sinister to his enemies in that superstitious age. The Cardinal made ample provision for his cats – fourteen of them – in his will, but he was no sooner dead than his Swiss guards rounded up the poor creatures and burned them.

In spite of all this, puss had managed to enter European legend. Every child now knows the story of Dick Whittington and his marvellous cat, and Perrault immortalized his French counterpart when he wrote down and gave literary form to the old story of *Le maître chat ou le chat botté,* known to the English-speaking world as *Puss in Boots.* And reason eventually prevailed; with the morbid fear of withcraft gone, man and cat settled down together. Hodge, Samuel Johnson's much-loved cat, was famous among his wide circle of friends, and thereafter the cat is found to be the valued friend of writers everywhere. Not a Blue Persian, or an Abyssinian, or a Seal Point Siamese – the breed is rarely mentioned. Probably they were just ordinary cats, as pretty and graceful and affectionate as even the most ordinary cat can be.

In ancient America the cats, great and small, had an honoured place. In Mexico there was a guild of Aztec

A Peruvian puma mask of about sixth Century AD *(left).*

Kittens instinctively use the fighting technique of all wild animals *(right).* The kitten on the left has forestalled an ambush and promptly caught his ambusher with a paw. He will next go for his neck in playful attack. Only fully grown toms actually do each other damage.

knights whom the Spanish chroniclers called the Knights Tiger – the creature which they called the tiger being the small, beautiful ocelot. The knights were not warriors but initiates in a mystical order striving for illumination. The ocelot was the creature that called a greeting to the sun – they could hear it at every dawn – and it was the sun that ruled their lives. The ocelot was the animal of the Fifth Sun, the age in which the Aztecs were living at the time of the Conquest. The age before that, the Fourth Sun, was that of the jaguar and scholars believe, on the evidence of the precious and elusive jaguar masks, that there was in earlier times a powerful jaguar cult.

In South America the traces are ubiquitous but the records existed only verbally. The destruction of the high Andean civilization by the Spaniards destroyed all hope of our ever learning the true details of the Andean way of life – what the recurring feline images can have meant we can only guess. Jaguars and pumas can be seen on pottery, in carvings, woven into the exquisite textiles, beaten into gold. That the great cats were cult animals seems certain but that is all that can be said. It is not surprising that they were, since they are beyond question the most majestic and beautiful creatures of the New World.

The small cats of America, the ocelots and margays, are exquisite creatures, not much bigger than our domestic cats and with markings in their warm brown – almost magenta-coloured – fur that make a striking effect. They are easily tamed and playful and one can imagine them gracing the homes of the Aztec and Inca families. We will never know if they did.

Now they are becoming popular as pets and it may be that puss, the queen of every household she enters, is due for yet more strains to add to her present colours and sizes. That she herself will never really change her nature we can be quite sure, and every cat-lover will be glad of it.

CARING FOR YOUR PET

To many people a cat is just a small furry animal useful for catching rats and mice, and that is all. To others it is a member of the household and a charming and decorative companion. There are also those who have never owned a cat in their lives but, because of changed circumstances or loneliness, or perhaps a move to a house with a garden, consider having one but hesitate as they know so little about the attention needed. It is with these people in mind that this chapter is written.

It is as well to weigh up carefully the advantages and disadvantages of ownership before taking on any animal. A kitten, like most pets, is a big responsibility and will need constant care and regular feeding. He will have to be house-trained, with litter trays changed frequently, and his food will have to be prepared and given at regular hours. He will require grooming and, above all, time must be found to play with him and show him affection. At holiday times, even if he is only to be left for a day or so, arrangements will have to be made for his welfare; young kittens cannot be left on their own for many hours, and adult cats too need companionship. If you are out at work all day but still feel you cannot live without a kitten, a happy solution is to have two so they will be company for each other. Even then, kittens need to be fed several times a day, but you may find that it is possible for a neighbour to come in and give the midday meal and check that all is well.

These then are the disadvantages, although most owners do not regard them as such, finding pleasure in looking after their pets.

The advantages are many. Cats do not need to be taken out for exercise, although they can be trained to walk on a lead if so desired. Being small in size they are not big eaters and if neutered they are quiet, unobtrusive and affectionate companions.

Cats appreciate a garden, but many live happily in apartments and get sufficient exercise from chasing a ball around. They all love sleeping in the sun and if there is a small balcony suitable for this it should be wired in, if high up, as cats do not always land on their feet as commonly supposed, and a fall from a height may result in a broken limb or may even be fatal. If there is no balcony, a small wire frame could be made to fit the window exactly, so that it may be left open in warm weather.

Barring accidents cats live a long time, thirteen or fourteen years on average, but twenty or more being known, so if you decide to take on the responsibility of a kitten, choose with care and make sure that you get what you really want. Should money be a consideration, mongrel kittens are very inexpensive; but if you yearn for a decorative Siamese, a square Short-haired British or Exotic, or an aristocratic Persian, the price will be very much more.

Unless breeding is being considered, there is really no necessity to be dogmatic as to the sex of the kitten. Neutering is fairly simple these days and castrating a male costs comparatively little, while the spaying of a female is rather more expensive. Nevertheless, some animal welfare societies are prepared to help towards the cost of spaying if it is more than can be afforded.

The easiest way to determine the sex of a kitten is to hold it in the hand and look under the tail. A male kitten has a circular anus near the base of the tail, with rudimentary testicles about half an inch away, while the female has a circular anus with a small slit, the entrance to the vagina, positioned very close to the anus under the tail.

It is far better for kittens that are to be kept purely as pets to be altered or neutered. A male will certainly be most affectionate when he is at home, but as he reaches maturity, he will want to follow his natural instincts and call on all the female cats in the district or even further afield, probably coming home battle-scarred and starving. If kept in the house he will spray on the walls and curtains, leaving his strong and unpleasant odour everywhere.

A female will start calling, or be on heat, or come into season, at any age from about five months. The first heat is unmistakable with most females. She will tread up and down on the ground with her back legs, making loud howling noises, and be even more affectionate than usual. She may try to get out to look for a mate, and visiting males will certainly soon be waiting hopefully outside. Should she succeed in finding a male, the gestation period is approximately 65 days.

The recommended age for altering or spaying is about three and a half months for a male and four and a half for a female, dependent on development. These ages apply to Britain. In the United States it is suggested that it should be done after the first heat for the female and at about eight months for the male, but professional advice should be sought as to the best time for a particular kitten.

It may not always be easy to find a kitten when you want one. With so many female cats being spayed, mongrel kittens are not as plentiful as they used to be, which is a very good thing as there are fewer strays.

If you are travelling with your pet – to the vet, to a show or on holiday – you will find that a basket like this one (*right*) is particularly useful.

They may be advertised in local newspapers or on advertisement boards outside pet shops, or be given away by friends only too eager to find good homes. The animal welfare societies in many countries are usually looking for suitable homes for unwanted cats and kittens.

If you prefer a pedigree kitten, it is a good idea to visit a cat show to see the various breeds and possibly order one while there. *Fur and Feather* (Idle, Bradford, Yorks), a weekly periodical, and *Cats* (66, The Dale, Widley, Portsmouth), a bi-monthly magazine, in Britain; *Cats* (Washington, Pa) and *International Cat Fancy* (641, Lexington Avenue, New York), in the United States carry advertisements for pedigree cats and kittens.

Before buying a kitten visit, if possible, the home where he was born and see the conditions under which he has been raised, making sure that both mother and kittens look happy and healthy. The kitten you finally choose should be at least nine to ten weeks old, with a full set of milk teeth, fully weaned, used to a small variety of food, and house-trained. He should be lively, steady on his legs, able to run freely, with tail held high. His eyes should be wide open, bright and sparkling, and inside the ears should be quite clean, with no smell or discharge. The nose should be cool to the touch and not running. There should be no signs

of diarrhoea under the tail, nor should there be any flea dirts, looking like black specks, in the coat. The fur should be springy to the touch, not lank and clinging. If you are buying a pedigree kitten as a pet, it will not matter if the ears are too big (if a Persian) or too small (if a Siamese), as a perfect show specimen is really only important from a breeding or exhibiting point of view, and such small faults will in no way detract from the appearance or the charm of the kitten. It is essential that he should be inoculated against feline infectious enteritis, and if not already done by the breeder this should be attended to as soon as the kitten has settled in; until then he should be kept indoors and away from other cats.

It is not necessary to buy expensive equipment for your pet. There are some very good cat baskets available, but most kittens sleep perfectly happily in a low

Few kittens are born at the cost of their mother's life but if it happens, the owner must be prepared to take full responsibility for it. The blind kitten (*above*) is being fed with a made-up substitute for its mother's milk – cow's milk will not do – given through a doll's bottle.

The Blue Point Siamese (*above right*) is about to lift her kitten by gripping a loose fold of skin on its neck. However, humans should not pick up a kitten by the scruff of the neck alone, as this may damage the muscles.

cardboard or wooden box with a blanket and newspaper in the bottom. It should be placed in a corner well away from draughts and raised slightly from the floor.

Whether pedigree or mongrel, all cats need grooming and should have their own small soft brush and suitable combs. Some playthings such as a small ball or rubber mouse should be provided.

A kitten should never be bought as a pet for a very small child. It is difficult for a mother to keep a constant watch to see that there is no mishandling, and as the bones of a kitten are very fragile they are easily bent or broken by hugging and squeezing, and the tail may be broken by pulling.

On arriving at his new home the kitten should be put in a room with the windows closed and the fireplace and chimney covered, as in these days of central heating he may never have seen a fire and may consider the chimney a means of escape – with disastrous results! A litter tray should be ready, as he may need to use it after his journey. There are some excellent plastic litter trays available, but an oven pan will do just as well. It should be low enough for the kitten to get into and out of with ease, and should be filled with earth, or a proprietary cat litter, ashes, peat moss, or even torn-up newspaper. Be sure to change the contents frequently, as cats are fastidious animals, refusing to use smelly trays. The tray should always be kept in the same spot, so that the kitten knows where to go. If a garden is available, he can be taken out there under guard once he has settled in.

When he first arrives he may be nervous and a little miserable in strange surroundings, missing his mother and brothers and sisters. He should be allowed to wander around the room as he pleases, and should not be fussed over unduly. If there is a dog or another cat in the house, it should not be left with the new kitten for the first few days, until it is clear that they are really friendly. Patience may be needed to achieve this, and to avoid jealousy care must be taken not to make too much of the new arrival in front of the older pets.

If there is a child in the house, he must be taught that a small kitten needs plenty of sleep, and also that the kitten should not be regarded as a toy to be picked up and pulled about. The child should be shown the correct way to hold the kitten, with one hand under and around the back and the other under the chest. A kitten must never be picked up by the back of the neck, as this may damage the muscles. Mother cats carry their kittens this way only when they are very small.

If the kitten has come from a breeder, the diet sheet provided should be adhered to closely for the first few days, and any new items should be introduced gradually. Milk should be given only very sparingly, if at all. Some kittens, particularly Siamese, are quite unable

17

to tolerate milk and suffer from diarrhoea if given it to drink. If there are no ill-effects it can be included in the diet, but remember, it is a food; clean water should always be available for drinking.

A kitten of nine or ten weeks requires four or five small meals a day at regular times. Starting with a tablespoonful at each meal, the amounts may be increased slightly each week, and the number of meals cut down, until at the age of six or seven months he is having three meals a day. By the time he is nine months old, two meals a day should be sufficient.

Cats are carnivorous, so meat, especially raw, is an essential feature of the diet. Fish is not, but some should be included to provide variety. Too much fish, or a diet of fish alone, may produce a form of eczema.

All food given to small kittens should be cut up small or minced, as they can choke on large chunks. The following may be included in the diet:

Beef (*raw or cooked*)

Rabbit (*cooked*)
Chicken (*cooked*)
Lamb (*cooked*)
Heart (*raw or cooked*). Only as part of a mixed diet, as too much may cause a mineral deficiency.
Horsemeat (*cooked or raw*). Only that offered for human consumption.
Liver (*cooked or raw*). Too much raw liver may cause diarrhoea.
Kidneys (*cooked or raw*)
Tongues (*cooked*)
Veal (*cooked*)
White fish (*cooked and with bones removed*)
Strained baby foods
Baby cereals
Tinned pilchards
Tinned salmon
Tinned sardines
Tinned herrings

Cooked vegetables, such as peas, beans or carrots, may be added to the meal if liked. A few cornflakes or a similar cereal, or brown bread, should be added to provide roughage. Cows' or tinned milk can be given if tolerated. Canned cat foods are a good standby and it is as well to include some in the diet so that the cat is used to them; but they should not be given to very young kittens as they can be too rich.

A large raw beef bone may be given especially to help when teething, but cooked bones should never be given. Chicken and rabbit bones cooked or raw should always be avoided as they can splinter and cause internal injuries. A few drops of a vitamin oil should be added to the food daily during the winter. Uneaten food should never be left in the cat's dish, particularly in the summer, as it can become stale or fly-infested and cause gastric enteritis.

Grass is a natural emetic and should always be available as it helps the cat bring up any hair swallowed, preventing furball. If there is no garden, grass can be grown indoors quite easily in a pot.

Although cats seem to spend a lot of time washing themselves, they also need careful grooming to rid the coat of dust and dirt and any loose hairs that may be licked down and cause furball.

It is as well to start the grooming the day after the kitten arrives so that he becomes used to being handled, and if he is played with for a short time afterwards, the grooming period will soon be looked forward to with pleasure. A fairly soft bristle brush, not a wire one, and two steel combs will be necessary, one with very fine teeth to catch the odd flea that may be picked up, and one with wider teeth for daily combing. Naturally a long-haired cat will need more attention than one with short hair, but the general procedure is the same. First feel through the coat to make sure there are no prickles or burrs, and tease out any tangles with the fingers. Comb and brush all over, placing the kitten flat on his back in your lap to do the stomach. Finish with hard hand stroking if you have a short-haired kitten, or with brushing up the fur, particularly round the face, if you have a long-haired kitten. Any dirt in the corner of the eyes should be wiped away gently with cotton wool, as should any dust in the ears. If the coat is neglected, and bad matts and tangles form, it may be necessary to cut these away with round-ended scissors, taking care not to pull or cut the skin. The cat's appearance

It is important that a cat has its own box or basket to sleep and play around in (*left and above right*). Line it with newspaper and a blanket and place it well away from draughts and raised slightly from the floor.

Another essential piece of your cat's equipment is a scratching post. This Tabby Point Siamese (*right*), like all cats, likes to flex his muscles on the post and also uses it to get rid of old sheaths on the claws.

19

will suffer for a while but the fur will soon grow again.

Training should start as soon as the kitten has settled down. Most kittens soon learn to use their litter trays, and if there is an occasional accident he should never be smacked but shown the spot, spoken to sharply and taken and put on the tray. If there is a garden that he is able to go in, he should at first be taken out under escort, but very soon he will be able to go out alone. If he has been using a litter tray it could be moved a little nearer the door each day, eventually being placed outside and then removed altogether when he uses the garden. Unfortunately some cats become so used to having a tray that they come in from the garden to use it.

The kitten should never be allowed to claw on the furniture and any attempt to do so should be stopped immediately. A sharp reprimand is better than smacking, as the animal will not realize it is a punishment and will just think he is being cruelly treated. The kitten should be shown where he is allowed to claw, and if you have no garden with a tree, you can buy from most pet shops special scratching posts for this purpose. Alternatively, a large log or string wound round the leg of the kitchen table will be quite suitable.

It is sometimes an advantage to have your cat used to a lead, and training for this should start when the kitten is about three months old. Most pet shops or animal welfare societies sell elastic collars and leads which are suitable for young kittens, although harnesses can be used when the cat is fully grown. Patience will be needed and also plenty of time, with the collar and lead being put on for a few minutes only for the first few days until the kitten is used to it. The first time walking on a lead is attempted the kitten will probably sit down and refuse to move, but eventually he will get the idea and will walk a few steps. Increase the distance slightly each day until, by the end of a few weeks, you will be able to take him out with you for short walks.

A lead is useful if you wish to take your pet in the car with you, as no cat should be allowed complete freedom in this situation. Accidents have been caused by the cat jumping unexpectedly on to the back of his owner, or getting under his feet when the brakes are being applied.

Most cats can be trained to do a few simple tricks, although being such independent creatures they will only do them when they feel like it and not to order. Many will retrieve paper balls thrown for them time and time again, their owners tiring before they do. Some enjoy hide-and-seek and will search for a small hidden toy, while others hide away, pouncing on their owners with glee as they walk by. They teach themselves to beg, open cupboards and refrigerators, turn on taps and open doors. They can be very affectionate, putting both paws round their owners' necks and licking their faces. Being highly intelligent, sensitive animals, they dislike being laughed at, scolded or shouted at, and will sulk if offended. Pleasure is expressed by purring, padding up and down with the paws (known as 'kneading the dough') and closing the eyes as if smiling when spoken to.

A few general remarks regarding travel may be helpful here. It is not generally realized that to prevent the introduction of rabies cats do not have freedom of movement into and out of Britain, although this does not apply to the United States. Any cat leaving Britain and then returning has to spend a period of six months in strict isolation in a quarantine cattery.

In Britain cats are allowed in containers on buses and coaches only at the conductor's discretion. On trains they may travel accompanied or unaccompanied, but must again be in an adequate container.

If you are unable to take your pet with you on holiday it may be necessary to find a good boarding cattery to take him to. Make an inspection of the cattery before booking and see the actual house and run your pet will occupy. It may be necessary to book up months in advance, so do not leave it too late. You will probably be asked to supply a certificate stating that your cat has been inoculated against feline infectious enteritis, and you may also have to supply a vet's certificate stating that the animal is in good health.

Owning a cat not only means seeing that he has a good varied diet, daily grooming and plenty of affection without being pampered, but also means making sure that he is fit. Fortunately the majority of cats are healthy animals, and barring accidents rarely need the services of a vet. Living in close association with a cat should enable the owner to detect very quickly when all is not well. Cats go down so rapidly that it is false economy to doctor your pet yourself, when possibly immediate treatment with antibiotics may mean the difference between life and death. It is important to telephone the vet at once with brief details of the cat's symptoms, and he will advise. If it comes to nothing no harm has been done but, should something serious be developing, you may have cut the length of the illness considerably by early treatment. If cost has to be considered, many of the animal welfare societies run animal clinics.

There are two major illnesses which affect kittens and cats. One is feline infectious enteritis or panleucopenia, which is a killer, invariably proving fatal once it has been contracted. It need not be, as inoculations are available which give practically one hundred per cent protection. Several vaccines are available, usually given in the form of two injections, but your vet will advise as to the best one, and the right age at which it should be given, usually when the kitten is about ten weeks old.

Feline infectious enteritis can kill in a matter of

It is rare for cats to enjoy walking for long on a lead (*above*), but it is certainly possible to train them to accept a collar and walk calmly if they are introduced to it as young kittens. This can be very useful at certain times, such as on journeys and in cars.

hours, with poison being blamed rather than an illness. The symptoms are generally a high fever, loss of appetite, slight vomiting, general lassitude and dehydration. The kitten may sit with his head over a bowl of water without drinking, or may crouch in a dark corner uninterested in anything. The vet should be called in at once as minutes count at the onset of this illness and the only hope is immediate treatment.

The virus is so violent that no new kitten should be introduced into a home where this illness has been present until at least six months afterwards, and then he should have been inoculated at least three or four weeks before. The premises should have been thoroughly disinfected, and the cat's blankets, basket, toys and so on destroyed. All contact with other cats and cat owners should be avoided, even to the extent of not writing letters from an infected household.

The other most serious illness is pneumonitis, also known as cat flu or distemper. It can cause death but it responds to early treatment with antibiotics. The symptoms are running eyes and nose, sneezing, wheezing, possibly diarrhoea, high temperature and refusal of food. There are a number of illnesses of a similar

respiratory nature under this heading and the symptoms may vary. The illness may be long and recovery slow, but careful nursing and a nourishing diet should effect a complete cure. If necessary, the animal may have to be given injections and be force-fed to keep him alive. A small quantity of glucose dissolved in warm water and given in the side of the mouth with a medicine dropper may help to keep him going.

Some vets vaccinate against pneumonitis but, as the illness is known in so many forms, it may be difficult to find the correct antidote.

Nursing is important in all cases of illness, as cats become very depressed and will give up easily. The patient should be isolated in a warm but not overheated room, and given a cardboard box lined with old blankets to sleep on, all of which should be destroyed when the cat has recovered. He must not be left alone for long but visited frequently, and talked to cheerfully. The owner should wear an overall when going into the room, changing his shoes and washing his hands afterwards. To make the cat feel more comfortable any mucus from the nose should be wiped away, and the areas around the mouth and under the tail washed with slightly dampened cotton wool.

Once the patient begins to recover, he should be tempted with tiny morsels of his favourite food. It may be necessary to push a little into his mouth so that he gets the taste. In some illnesses the sense of smell may be lost, so something with a strong flavour, such as tinned pilchards, should be tried at first; anything to get him to start eating again of his own accord.

There are various contingencies which may occur during a cat's lifetime, as follows:

Abscess An abscess may develop after a fight with another cat, and is caused by a puncture of the skin that is so small that it passes unnoticed until the cat looks miserable and goes off his food. Close examination will reveal a hard, shining swelling, which gradually grows larger. This is filled with pus and may have to be brought to a head with thrice-daily hot water fomentations – hot but not boiling. Professional treatment is recommended as the vet may consider antibiotic injections necessary. The fur should be cut short around the swelling, and lancing may be needed with a sterilized needle when the swelling has come to a head. Once the pus is out, the cat will be in much less pain and should start eating. The wound should not be allowed to close up too quickly as the abscess may redevelop.

Bites During a fight a cat may be bitten, and any such wound should be bathed with a mild disinfectant to prevent sepsis.

Broken bones A bone may be broken should a cat be hit by a car, receive a blow, or fall from a height. If this is suspected, keep the cat warm and as still as possible, and call in the vet immediately.

Constipation This may occur due to change of diet when the kitten goes to his new home, or it may be due to underfeeding or his food being too dry. A small teaspoonful of corn or mineral oil may effect a cure, but if it is persistent, professional advice must be sought, as it may be caused by a furball or a blockage.

Diarrhoea This may happen with a change of home, and may be due to excess of milk, wrong or too wet feeding. In the summer a frequent cause is fly-infected food. All food should be withheld and water only given to drink, and if the condition continues for more than a day the vet should be consulted, as it may be the start of severe illness.

Ear trouble Sitting with the head on one side, pawing at the ears, or shaking the head may be the first indication of ear trouble. Close inspection may show a dark brown discharge with an unpleasant smell, indicating the presence of ear mites, generally referred to as canker. As there are various types, a vet should be consulted to prescribe the correct treatment.

Eye trouble Some cats with very short noses have a brown discharge in the corners of the eyes which should be wiped away daily so that the face is not permanently stained.

If the cat paws at his eyes which are severely inflamed and have a sticky discharge, he may be suffering from conjunctivitis, which is contagious and should be treated professionally.

Fleas Many cats pick up an occasional flea, but should never be allowed to become infested, as having fleas and tape worms go together. The daily grooming should ensure that any odd flea is discovered, but should the fur be full of tiny black specks, which are the dirts, a suitable insecticide must be used, following the procedure given on the container. No insecticides should be used on kittens or nursing mothers as any licked down can cause the death of small animals.

Poisoning A cat may become fatally ill through licking or swallowing substances which are poisonous to them, such as weed-killers or flea powders containing DDT, or eating rats that have been poisoned. Aspirin should never be given to a cat as this is also a poison. As treatment depends entirely on the type of poisoning, the symptoms should be telephoned to the vet immediately. In an emergency a piece of washing soda pushed down the cat's throat, or making him drink some salt water may induce sickness thereby saving his life.

Skin trouble There are several skin complaints from which a cat may suffer. These include eczema, which is frequently caused by an allergy, mange and ringworm, both the latter being contagious. Any bare patches in the fur, particularly round ones, should be suspect and veterinary treatment is essential.

A cat uses his tongue as sponge, brush and comb, but for those parts of his body that he cannot reach he will use his paws which he first moistens (*above right*).

By the time kittens are old enough to leave their mother, they will have learned to be cautious. Like this Tabby (*below*), they will stay behind cover while sizing up not only any danger but also their own line of retreat.

Stings   Although the fur usually gives adequate protection, cats may be stung through patting at a bee or a wasp. If possible, pull out the sting and dab the place with a mild disinfectant. A sting in the mouth and throat with much swelling must be treated as serious, necessitating urgent veterinary treatment.

Teething   At about the age of five or six months the second teeth begin to appear, and the milk teeth fall out. If the kitten goes off his food, examine his gums – you may find that they are inflamed. A daily dose of milk of magnesia and easily eaten food should be given. He may have to be encouraged to eat with tiny pieces of his favourite food.

In an older cat dribbling or bad breath may be a sign of bad teeth or tartar, both of which can easily be dealt with by the vet.

Round worms   Worms in cats and kittens cause debility, loss of weight and even anaemia. A kitten with worms may have a coat that looks in poor condition, a swollen belly and bad breath. Worms may be vomited or seen in the motions, like thin pieces of string. Round worms are far more serious in kittens than adults, and the vet should be asked to prescribe the correct tablets for the size, weight and age of the animal. Not all kittens suffer from worms and it is not necessary to worm as a matter of course; in fact, it can be very dangerous. Indiscriminate worming-out has been

known to cause the death of small animals.

Tape worm   If a cat has a large appetite but still looks thin and in poor condition, a tape worm should be suspected. This is serious, causing anaemia, debility, even fits. Segments of the flat worm may be seen hanging from the cat's anus or sticking to his fur like dried segments of rice grains. Fleas act as the intermediary host to the tape worm, so if there are fleas in his coat a cat may also suffer from a tape worm. As the head attaches itself to the intestines, with the body growing up to several feet in length, it is essential that the correct medicine prescribed by the vet is given to ensure that the whole worm is expelled without doing internal damage. After treatment, it may be necessary to give extra raw meat to counteract anaemia.

The foregoing are the minor ailments which *may* affect your pet – but fortunately rarely do, as apart from inoculations and neutering many cats never have to visit a vet.

The way your cat's personality develops will depend on you and on his upbringing and, although to you he may seem almost human, it should be remembered that the cat is a domestic animal and as such should be allowed to live as far as possible a life of his own, without pampering or undue fuss. Treated and fed correctly, you will have the pleasure of his company for many a long year.

THE CHARACTER OF CATS

Cats are as individual as people and of all household pets, they are undoubtedly the most independent. Unlike dogs, cats can never be made to do anything to which they object. It is often said that some dogs and their owners are so devoted to each other that they take on each other's personality and sometimes even look alike. Although cats can be just as devoted, they rarely take on an owner's personality – they have enough of their own.

Many cats can perform clever tricks and can open doors, windows and cupboards with dexterity. Siamese and Burmese are particularly agile; they will beg, retrieve and perform wonderful dances and jumps when they find suitable playthings.

Cats like to be flattered and to be told they are beautiful and clever; it is certain they understand what is said, and they react very definitely to anger. Cats dislike high voices and violent noises; they like flowers and are attracted by bright colours.

Cats communicate more than most animals with humans and with each other by the way they move their ears and tails. They have many eloquent facial expressions and can portray disapproval, fear, anger, pleasure and many other emotions. Cats' voices are most expressive, and can indicate all the various moods. They can be demanding, cajoling, bullying or merely conversational; they leave you in no doubt when they are hungry, cross or disapproving, and equally there is no mistaking their purr of happiness, a sound made only by cats, large and small. A Siamese in season has to be heard to be believed and the Burmese is almost as noisy. Most other breeds are quieter; some are almost silent and have to be watched closely if you do not want them to get out and find their own mate. When males fight the noise is frightful, reminiscent of the jungle.

Except for some white cats which are born deaf, cats' hearing is acute, and their ears will pick up the slightest sound. Ears also indicate a cat's mood; a flick acknowledges that you have been heard, but when the ears are flattened and lie close to the head, it is a danger signal and it is advisable not to handle a cat when in such a mood. When a cat is angry it fluffs its tail out to twice the normal size, and a ridge of fur standing up along the spine shows that it is more than ready to fight.

Never laugh at cats because they hate it, although they are always more than willing to make fun of their owners, and Siamese and Burmese in particular have a great sense of humour.

Cats walk on their toes, and are notorious for their ability to walk completely silently. They can do this because they retract, or draw in, their claws, all except the Siamese, that is – their claws are unretractable, like those of the dog. Consequently, they do not walk silently and are not adept at landing softly in a small space.

It is said that cats can see in the dark. Although this fact has been disputed, it is certain that both wild and domestic cats hunt at night.

As cats are clean and fastidious, you should help to keep their coats free from fleas and their ears clean, or they will be very miserable and unhealthy.

Cats can be very brave and there are many stories of instances when they have awakened people to warn them of fire, leaking gas or floods. They are particularly courageous when they have kittens, and if danger threatens they will go to the greatest lengths to get them to a safe place.

One of the most famous cats was one that lived through the London air raids of the last war, a small Tabby and White called Faith. She had walked into St Augustine's Church in Watling Street as a stray kitten, and as she was never claimed, the Rector took her to live in the Rectory House adjoining the Church. In September 1940 Faith had a kitten called Panda, and the two of them were comfortably settled on the top floor of the Rectory House. Later that month, however, the cat became restless and eventually took the kitten out of the basket and installed it in a room three floors below at the other side of the house.

When the Rector found the empty basket he searched for the cats and took them upstairs. Faith at once seized the kitten and took it downstairs again. The Rector took the kitten upstairs four times and then gave up the struggle. Three nights later the blitz began and a bomb went through the roof of the Rectory house. The Rector returned to find his house a mass of burning ruins, but in spite of firemen saying it was hopeless, he started to search for the cat. He called Faith several times, and to his relief he heard a faint cry in answer. Peering down he saw the brave cat entirely hemmed in by rubble, the kitten between her paws. He hacked a passage out of the debris and then coaxed the cat and her kitten out. Both were begrimed but unhurt. Faith was taken to the Church vestry just before the whole house collapsed in ruins. There she calmly settled down with her kitten, knowing they were safe, which indeed they were, as the Church was not hit. She was the first cat to win decorations for courage.

That this Tabby (*right*) wants something is evident in the line of his head and the arch of his back. Cats are expressive creatures and they can portray their many moods with their voices, eyes, ears and even tails.

The Foreign White (*right*) demonstrates clearly that the cat is built for great speed. Although it is most often seen lazily relaxing, this is because it is really a nocturnal animal. When the cat is hunting it moves quickly and silently, covering the ground in great leaps, the line of the back staying parallel to the ground. The way the cat runs is similar to the giraffe or camel. First the front and back legs on one side move, then the front and back legs on the other. This is what gives the smooth gliding movement, unlike other animals which appear to jog along.

The old saying 'Curiosity killed the cat' is far from true, for the cat is a cautious animal (*left and below*). Without doubt it is an inquisitive creature but it would not take unnecessary risks to satisfy that curiosity. It will venture into new ground only after it has surveyed the landscape and taken full stock of the situation (*below right*). However, it is not a timid creature. Unlike the dog, which will usually rush off in the face of danger, the cat will stand its ground. By arching its back to make itself look bigger than it really is, snarling, hissing and spitting, it looks a formidable opponent. Most dogs will not stay to face such a bundle of fury.

All cats love to laze in the sun (*far left*). If you do not have a garden or balcony, a wire frame can be easily made to fit a window, so that it can be left open in warm weather.

'Cool cats everywhere – I should like to make a protest on behalf of cats in cartoons who are badly treated by mice. This nonsense gives a false view of the intelligence of our kind and I should like to make a formal declaration to this effect.

'If we are able to make our voice heard, we must all howl together. There is tremendous loss of face for our species whenever one member is outwitted by a mere mouse, which is in any case an impossibility.

'I realize that this kind of humour is popular but I am sure you will all agree with me when I say that we cats do not like being laughed at. Like all of my friends, I enjoy a good joke, but this has really gone too far.

'I am not making this speech out of any desire to become famous, nor do I resent not having been invited to take a star part in a film. We cats must stand together or before we know where we are someone will write a story about a cat being frightened by a spider.

'If you would like to become a member of my organization for the Preservation of the Dignity of Cats, my secretary will be pleased to send you details. Thank you all for your kind attention.'

Cats love to laze or romp in grass (*left and below*). They love the gentle movement as it is caught in the breeze, they enjoy hunting the insects that abound in the undergrowth, and they like to eat grass too, as this is a natural medicine. For town cats with no access to a grassy patch it is important to provide grass grown in pots or boxes. Crow's-foot grass seems to be a great favourite and a fresh supply should be sown every week or ten days.

Although cats enjoy climbing trees, it is really part of their instinctive caution that makes them find a place where they can be safe from intrusion and can watch for anything stirring below, like this little kitten (*right*).

This kitten (*left*) may only be small but its claws are strong. Being curved and very sharp, they are well adapted for the cat to grasp its prey or for it to get a firm grip on a smooth surface when it is climbing. The claws can be extended or retracted by means of flexor tendons. When the claws are not in use they are hidden in openings at the end of the digits so that they are protected from wear and tear, thus remaining sharp for when they are needed.

Cats cannot bear to feel anything messy or sticky in their coats and, being naturally fastidious, they will spend a great deal of time washing and cleaning themselves (*right*). The tongue of the cat is covered with rasp-like protuberances which give it that rough feeling and enables the cat to lick its coat clean. It is wise, however, to groom all domestic cats every day, as it is very good for them and many also enjoy it.

With their instinct for providing themselves with comfort and warmth, these little kittens (*below*) have found an unusual spot beneath a radiator. Here they can sleep, feeling secure and protected.

The white cat (*left*) is probably very similar to that owned by the Prophet Mohammed long ago in Arabia. It is written that, while Mohammed preached from the tallest minaret in Mecca, his cat, which he called Muezza, would sleep in the sleeve of his robes.

Although cats like their own box or basket, they will sleep anywhere and in the most awkward positions. This white cat (*below*) looks as if he might wake up with a headache.

It is thought that black cats with orange eyes may have been introduced into the mating pattern to transfer the orange eyes to the white cats. It is difficult to achieve a really vivid orange but it is very striking when it does occur, as in this cat (*right*).

CHOOSING A CAT

If you are thinking of buying a pedigree kitten for a pet, or perhaps with a view to breeding and showing, make your choice carefully. If you live in a flat or house in a built-up area, it is often best to choose a placid British Short-haired kitten as they are contented, easy to manage and, if neutered, will grow into handsome cats. You will need more time to look after a Long-hair, as their coats require very careful grooming. If you have a comparatively rare breed, your responsibilities are much greater unless you have it neutered or spayed. Some breeds need more exercise than others; one of these is the Abyssinian cat, which is very active and should be allowed plenty of freedom.

All the Orientals are great individualists, demanding attention and companionship as well as freedom. The Russian Blue has a quieter temperament and would be happy to spend most of its time indoors with its owner. Rex cats make excellent pets, being very tough and healthy, and give their owners a dog-like devotion. They are easy to manage and will eat anything. The Cornish type usually have thicker coats, but the Devon have the cute pixie expression which appeals to many people. Both the Cornish and the Devon Rex also make beautiful neuters. However, they can be jealous, a characteristic they share with Siamese cats, and if kept with other animals must never be overlooked.

All cats, however, need space and should not be overcrowded or they will not thrive; unlike dogs, they do not have the herd instinct and, unless brought up together, may really dislike one another. If you have adult cats and wish to introduce another, it is much wiser to get a kitten as after a short time the adult cats will accept it, but it is a difficult and tiring job to fit in an adult cat. In fact, it may never settle in at all.

Cats and kittens are inquisitive and will stray quite long distances. There is the danger that they may be killed on the roads, and in many areas the number of stolen cats is increasing, so safeguard your pet. Burmese in particular, probably the most playful and curious of all cats, have a tendency to wander away and have been known to be absent for days; sadly they do not always return.

You may not wish to own a pedigree kitten; you may be given a non-pedigree or you may fall for one in a pet shop, but whatever you have they all need the same care and attention.

If you are out all day, try to have two kittens, as they will be company for one another and will thrive better if not bored and lonely. It is wiser not to take kittens until they are at least ten weeks old, unless you can be around all the time to see that they get four small meals daily. If you intend to take up breeding, start in a small way with not more than two kittens, and then only if you are able to give your pets a great deal of attention. It is advisable to keep females to begin with and do not attempt to keep a male as a stud until you have experience of breeding. The most important thing is to find a good stud that will suit and complement your cat's breeding, especially if you want to breed kittens that will do well on the show bench and be strong and healthy. You can get advice about this, and do not think that because a cat is a champion you must use him; champions are often overworked.

Never leave your queen where the stud's quarters are grubby and where there is no adequate pen for the queen to live in until she is ready to mate. It is really best to visit the stud's home yourself and see the conditions he is living in. Do not let your queen have more than two litters in a year, especially if Burmese or Siamese, as they tend to have big litters of five, six and seven kittens, and females can become exhausted if allowed to breed every time they come into season. Incidentally, both these breeds can be very noisy, particularly when they call, and are not suitable if you live in a flat, as the noise will probably annoy other people in the house.

Cat breeding can be an interesting and absorbing hobby, provided one is not tempted to keep too many cats, and also is not dependent on selling the kittens, as it is often difficult to place them in suitable homes. They should be inoculated from the age of ten weeks, and not sold until this has been done.

If you cannot devote sufficient time to breeding, start with two neuters. They will be company for one another and if they are pedigree cats, can be registered and exhibited at shows in the neuter classes. If they are not pedigrees, they can be exhibited at any show which has Household Pet classes. These always create great interest, as there are Blacks, Whites, Tabbies of all colours, Blacks and Whites, Torties, Long-hairs and Short-hairs, and they are judged by well-known people. One cat is usually chosen as the Best Household Pet, and if there are several classes there will be a Best Long-hair and Best Short-hair. Classes for kittens will be available too, and these are always a great centre of attraction.

It is extremely difficult to resist a tiny kitten, especially one as appealing as this White Long-hair *(right)*. All too often people take on a kitten without stopping to consider how much attention it will need in the way of grooming, feeding and training.

On safari (*above*). This mother cat is giving her young ones a first lesson in hunting. The cat's reactions and perceptions are amazingly swift and acute. The picture shows clearly that although the kittens are nervous (this can be seen by the way they carry their tails), they are tense and ready for action. For them the big adventure is only just beginning.

One might think that a Tabby would have a problem in choosing a background to set off his colouring. This one (*left*) seems to have found the answer.

The true Manx is one with no tail whatsoever, and is called a Rumpy (*right*). However, there are Manx cats of pure breeding with a little bit of a tail, and these are called Stumpies. When two Rumpies are mated the kittens often die at birth but when Stumpies are introduced into the breeding pattern, this seems to eliminate the risk.

If you live in the country, chances are that your cat will collect burrs in its coat (*left*). It can also pick up parasites from the grass, particularly if there are hedgehogs about. It is important to see that the cat enjoys a vigorous brushing every day to remove these nuisances. Before combing, run your hand over the cat's body to remove burrs. A fine comb will get through to the under fur to remove parasites. Give the first brushing against the lie of the coat, from tail to head, to remove loose hairs, then brush the hair down with long, sweeping strokes.

The importance to cats of scratching is often underestimated. An ordinary log, complete with bark, like the one in the picture (*right*) is very suitable for this purpose but when prolonged use has worn it smooth, it should be replaced with another.

In order to enjoy their freedom, cats should be given access to the garden whenever they feel the need. The simplest way to do this is to have a cat door fitted to one of the outside doors of the house (*below right*). This will also obviate the need to send the cat out at night, which is unkind particularly in bad weather.

This family of Turkish Van cats (*left*) are obviously enjoying their basket. Once the kittens are more than three weeks old and are really beginning to grow, it does not matter so much what sort of basket they have, but it is important to give the mother a well-ventilated, draught-free, warm basket or box when she is about to produce the kittens, in the hope that she will consent to use it. Without proper guidance she will invariably make for your best hat or the airing cupboard.

Like all kittens, these five Siamese (*below*) are totally adorable. When they are born they are about the size of mice but they grow very quickly. When the kittens are about a month old they begin to climb out of their box. It is very distracting to have these little

42

charmers about and difficult to settle to serious matters. They like lots of attention, so talk to them quietly, for conversation is important. Kittens soon begin to understand the different tones of voice. Like babies they tire very quickly, and therefore require plenty of rest and sleep.

Long-haired cats, sometimes called Persians (*right*), tend to have rather small litters of kittens. The size may vary from one to six but most often the number produced is three and this is a comfortable number for the queen to rear. Long-haired cats are considered by many to be the most beautiful of all but the long, flowing coat does need a great deal of grooming and care.

One great advantage of owning a cat rather than a dog is that it does not need to be exercised, for play is itself the best form of exercise. A cat loves the freedom of a garden, for here it can romp in the grass and stretch its muscles (*left*).

When choosing a kitten (*above*), it is a good idea to see it first with its mother. This will give you an indication as to how it will look as an adult. It also provides a guide to the mother's health and the conditions under which the kittens have been reared. Before making your choice, watch the kittens at play, then go for one that is sturdy, full of life, with wide-open, bright and sparkling eyes.

Perhaps the best of the Tabbies, for type, is the Silver (*right*), an exquisite creature with jet black markings showing clearly against the pure silver ground colour and offset by clear, distinctively green eyes. Showy, yet shy and gentle, the Silver Tabby Short-hair has recently become very popular throughout the world, and classes at most shows are well filled with worthy examples of the variety.

The Tabby Point Siamese (*above*) is one of the more recent varieties to have appeared, and is very striking in colouring indeed. Siamese in general can sometimes look out of place when they are hunting outside in the grass, as their colouring makes them conspicuous.

Although it is a disputed fact that cats can see in the dark, they can certainly see better than most mammals in a dim light. The cat is a nocturnal animal so its eyes are adapted for hunting by moonlight (*above left*). Many animals that are about when we are asleep can increase the amount of light passing into the retina because they have a reflecting layer behind. It is this reflecting layer that causes a cat's eyes to shine at night when a bright light is directed at them. One of the reasons the Ancient Egyptians regarded the cat as sacred was because they thought their eyes reflected the sun while it was hidden from Man.

This kitten (*left*) has obviously got something very urgent and secret to tell its mother. It is believed that the cat's 'miaow' is reserved for their conversations with humans but when they talk to each other there are as many as a hundred different sounds and tones they can use.

This cat (*right*) has found himself a warm and comfortable spot. He lives at a brewery where horses are used to pull the drays, and the hay left for the horses' supper makes an attractive bed and playground.

47

THE POPULAR BREEDS

The English cats today consist of the Long-hairs or Persians, the British and Foreign Short-hairs and the Siamese. In the early days of the Cat Fancy the British Short-hair was the most numerous and popular; there were a few Angoras and a few Blue, Black, Red and Tabby Persians; Siamese were very rare and many of the breeds that are popular today were unknown.

The principal breeds are Long-haired: Black, White with blue or orange eyes, Blue, Red Self, Cream, Smoke, Tortoiseshell and Tortoiseshell and White, Blue Cream, Brown, Red and Silver Tabby, Chinchilla, Colourpoint and Bi-coloured. The latest additions are the Turkish cat, which is white with auburn markings, and the French blue-eyed Birman with Seal, Blue, Chocolate or Lilac Points. These two breeds have longer heads and noses and larger ears than the Long-hairs, and their coats are not so long, though their tails are as bushy. It is interesting to note that in Sweden Turkish cats are also found with Tortoiseshell, Red, and Tortoiseshell and White colouring; type is the same. These breeds are not yet as popular as the older ones, but numbers are gradually increasing.

Today the pedigree British Short-hair has declined in popularity but you can still see worthy representatives of most of the colour varieties in every show. Perhaps the most popular are Blacks, Whites, Silver Tabbies and Silver Spotteds. British Blues and Tortoiseshell and Whites, Creams, Blue Creams, Tortoiseshells, Brown and Red Tabbies and Bi-coloureds are rather scarce, although we are now seeing some excellent Brown Spotteds and Brown and Red Tabbies. Manx cats have phases of popularity; few have been seen recently but they will be back again. These clever and curious little cats are not money-makers and are kept only by people who really love the breed.

The Foreign Short-hairs are always around, although our oldest breeds, the Russian Blues and Abyssinians, are not very numerous. The most popular at the moment are the Brown Burmese, followed by the Blue Burmese. These were the only two colours until breeders imported two Champagne coloured cats from America and a Chocolate coloured one from Canada. Now other colours are appearing: Cream, Blue Cream and Lilac (known in America as Frost).

The Havanas are gaining in popularity and are an interesting breed of Siamese type with bright green eyes and a wistful expression. The best examples have coats the colour of a polished chestnut. The most recent recognitions are the Cornish and Devon Rex; they have fought their way up since the fifties and there are now the two separate varieties, with their own breed numbers and standard of points. There are a few Si-Rex, bred from a Siamese and a Rex; the good specimens are of Rex type, with blue eyes and the Seal Point colouring. The Foreign Whites have pure white coats and lovely blue eyes; of Siamese type, they have been mysteriously bred from British Whites, Siamese and Havanas. The Chartreux is a well-built cat of similar type to the British Blue. It is seen on the Continent and has a rather soft, dark blue coat and yellow eyes. The Lion-clawed or polydactyl cat, usually a Tabby, has six toes and is a very handsome and well-built cat.

The Cat Fancy in the USA recognizes the same breeds of cat as we do, though not always by the same name, as well as several more. The Colourpoint is known as the Himalayan, and there are many more colour varieties of the breed. The Russian Blue is known as the Maltese and the Tortoiseshell and White, both the Long-haired and the Short-haired versions, is known as the Calico cat. Angoras are to be found on the American show benches but not here. These cats are said to have originated from Angora in Western Asia, and were great favourites with the Turks. Many of our Long-haired Blues, Whites, Creams and Chinchillas are exported to the USA, together with Colourpoints and the French Birmans of the same type as the Turkish, with good blue eyes and white gloved feet.

The American Fancy recognizes the Peke-Faced Tabby, the Tortie Long-hair, the Shaded Silvers and the Maine Coon cats, which are a popular and distinctive breed. There is also a Long-haired Blue Tabby and the Kymer, which can really be described as a Long-haired Siamese, as type and colouring are similar. A great many other colours are recognized, such as the variously coloured Cameos, the Red Smokes, Self-Chocolates, Self-Lilacs, and the Tibetan Temple Cat, which rather resembles the Kymer.

Short-hairs follow the same coat patterns as the English cats: Black, White, Blue, Manx, Rex and Siamese. Another Blue is the Korat cat, said to have come from Thailand; it has a fairly heavy body, a heart-shaped mask and very brilliant yellow-green eyes. They are rather scarce, as efforts are made to keep the breed pure. Other breeds of cat advertised in American journals are Japanese Bobtails, Balinese, Egyptian Mau, Tonkinese with blue eyes, all fascinating cats, carefully maintained by the breeders.

The Red Abyssinian (*right*) is one of the cats to have recently received a class number and a standard of points. The black ticking is absent on the coat and the colour is a solid copper red. In the USA it is known as the Sorrel.

There are four varieties of Cameo cat (*left*): Shell, Shaded, Smoke and Tabby. It is recognized in the United States of America as a breed but not so in Britain. They conform to the standards for Long-hairs and the pattern is the same as that of Chinchilla and Silvers. The tipping on the long, pale coat is red to give a tinsel appearance.

This Long-haired Blue Cream cat (*below far left*) has a coat of excellent intermingled pastel shading. These cats are invariably female and are the result of cross-breeding between Blues and Creams. Breeders have worked out a breeding pattern so that the colours of the kittens are predictable. They are striking cats with orange eyes glowing against the misty effect of the coat.

The orange eyes of the Long-haired White cat (*below left*) indicate that it is not deaf. White cats have a tendency to deafness, particularly when they have blue eyes.

Burmese cats (*above right*) are now very popular in America and Britain. Originally, a female cat was taken from Burma to the United States in 1930 and was mated with a Siamese male. The males from the resulting litter were mated back to the mother and sired dark brown cats of Foreign type which became known as Brown Burmese. In order to establish a breed they had to breed true for several generations, so it was not until 1936 that these cats received official recognition in America. They arrived in Britain in the late 1940s but did not receive official status until 1952. The Burmese are less vocal than the Siamese, and also less nervous and highly strung. In fact, most Burmese are extremely placid and calm, and they are particularly intelligent and friendly.

In America the Odd-eyed White (*right*) has a breed class and number but in Britain it cannot be shown in a class of its own because it is not a recognized breed. These unusual cats are the result of a cross-mating between Blue-eyed Whites and Orange-eyed Whites, when the breeders have been endeavouring to breed out the tendency to deafness in white cats with blue eyes. Some owners of white cats with one blue eye and one orange eye believe that the cat can only hear on the side with the orange eye but there is no evidence to support this.

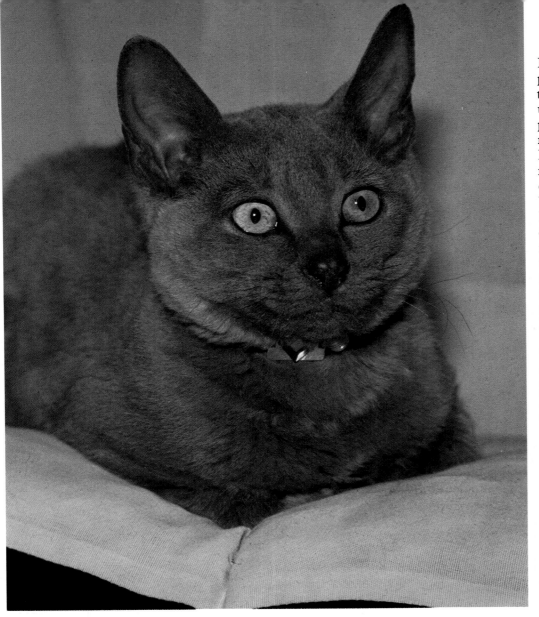

In 1950 on a farm in Cornwall a peculiar kitten appeared in a litter born to a Tortoiseshell mother and an unknown father. The kitten was peculiar because it had a curly coat – normally cats have straight hair. Because it was so unusual the owner mated it back with its mother. More curly kittens were the result and thus began the Cornish Rex breed (*left*). Less than ten years after the appearance of the Cornish Rex a curly coated kitten made its appearance in Devon. There was no connection between the two and successive experiments showed that they were the result of different genetic mutations. Now the Cornish and Devon Rex are separate established breeds.

The beautiful Red Spotted (*below*) is as old as time, but for some reason the pedigree died out early in this century. However, it is now making a second appearance and is increasing in numbers.

The coat of the Maine Coon cat (*right*) resembles that of a raccoon and the legs show a slight toeing-in rather like that animal, and it is from this that the cat gets its name. The head is pointed and the eyes often show a slight slant, even though the shape of the eyes is perfectly round. The Long-haired Tabbies that went to America with the early settlers are thought to be the ancestors of the Maine Coon cat.

The delicate colour effect of the Long-haired Smoke (*left*) is created by a white undercoat and a black topcoat which shades to silver on the sides and leaves a silver ruff and ear tufts. The undercoat shows clearly as the cat moves. A Blue Smoke is also recognized, and in America Smoke is recognized as a colour variety of other kinds of cat.

The Himalayan Cat of the United States (*below*), basically the same as the British Colourpoint, is a Persian cat to which the Siamese colouring has been transferred. Breeders in several countries experimented over a long period to obtain a long-haired Siamese. One of the most attractive features of the Siamese is its slim elegance, but this Foreign type did not look right with long hair. It took a long time to achieve the delicate Siamese colouring and at the same time eliminate the type.

One of the oldest of the pedigree breeds is the Black Long-haired cat (*right*). Unfortunately it has a coat which can easily become shabby, and it is very difficult to keep it in first class condition. The standard calls for the coat to be raven or jet black. Black cats who frequently get their feet wet as a result of walking through grass tend to get rusty marks about their paws and legs, and strong sunshine can have a bleaching effect on the coat.

The Korat (*below*) is a rare Siamese type of cat and its particular characteristic is its colouring. The coat is a solid slate blue with each hair silver-tipped, and the large, prominent eyes are bright green or amber. It actually comes from Thailand, where it is equally rare; a male and a female were taken to the United States and now Korats are beginning to make their appearance at the cat shows, having demonstrated that they can be bred successfully. These cats are of the Foreign type, and several generations of breeding true must pass before they can become an accepted breed.

This Jungle Cat (*above*) has been domesticated. In the United States of America some people like to keep exotic cats for pets. They come mostly from pet shops, as they are nearly always jungle-born; few are bred by cat fanciers. The most common are the Ocelot and Margay, which make very impressive and unusual pets.

The beauty of the Chinchilla (*left*) lies in its colouring. The breed is said to have originated from a crossing of Tortoiseshell with Silver Tabby, and this ancestry can be seen in the kittens, for they are born with tabby markings. As they grow, the markings disappear and the mature cat has a pure white undercoat, each hair tipped with black to give a sparkling, silver appearance.

The Manx cat (*below*) does not conform to the basic pattern of cats, since it has no tail, or if it does have one it is never more than half a tail. Since there has to be an explanation for all things, an assortment of legends exists to account for the Manx cat's loss. It has been said that Irish warriors removed the tails to decorate their shields and helmets. Rather than have this happen, the anxious mother cats bit off the tails of their kittens at birth. There is also a story that Noah cut the tail off the cat as he slammed the door of the Ark – the cat was the last animal to enter. Some tailless cats from Spain are supposed to have swum ashore after the Armada, and Manx cats are said to be descended from these. These stories merely convey that they are of unknown origin. There is no real evidence that they originated on the Isle of Man, although the Manx is featured on the reverse side of a coin in their currency.

The fully grown healthy Brown Burmese (*right*) is a beautiful example of the breed. The coat should be a solid, rich, dark seal brown, shading to slightly lighter on chest and belly. There should be no white or tabby markings. The ears, mask and points should be only a little darker than the back coat colour.

The true Bi-coloured cats are difficult to breed with the colour in the correct proportions and in the right places (*left*). The difficulty in achieving the correct pattern made these cats almost disappear from the shows. Fortunately they are making a comeback, and have just received recognition in Britain for a second time. Colours for the standard may be black, cream, blue or orange, all with white as the second colour.

The ground colour of the Tabby (*below*) is pure silver, and the kitten shows how the tail should be neatly ringed. The distinctness and correct placing of the marking is the most important feature in Tabby cats. It is also important to see that the colours are quite separate – the black must not become mixed with the ground colour.

Both the Long-haired and Short-haired Tortoiseshell and Whites are called Calico cats by New Englanders (*right*). Males are extremely rare and the breed cannot be produced to order, as the genetic pattern is unpredictable.

FROM THE ORIENT

When we talk of the breeds from the Orient, we mean the royal cats of Siam. With their inscrutable eyes of deep blue, their air of aloofness, their elegant bodies and their coats of sharply contrasting seal and fawn, they are unlike any other breed of cat. The original Seal Point is still a firm favourite, in spite of the many other colour variations now seen in the Siamese breed.

Siamese cats came into England officially in 1884; a pair was a gift from the King of Siam to Mr Owen Gould, then the Consul General at Bangkok. He later gave them to his sister, Mrs Veley, who bred from them and in time became a founder member of the Siamese Cat Club. Later two more were allowed to leave Siam for England, imported by Mrs Vyvyan and Miss Forester Walker. However, it is known that Siamese were exhibited at the Crystal Palace Show in 1871, and between that date and 1887 fifteen males and four females were shown. It would therefore appear that some had been smuggled into this country, in spite of the fact that the King of Siam was very concerned with true breeding and for many years allowed only a few cats to leave Bangkok with trusted people.

For several years breeders found these cats very delicate; they belonged exclusively to wealthy people who mistakenly coddled them, keeping them in overheated rooms and not allowing a breath of air to blow over them. They were incorrectly fed and very prone to intestinal disorders. Gradually, however, it was realized that Siamese were quite tough if they were allowed more freedom and fresh air, kept from draughts and damp, and fed sensibly. However, kittens always need special care and attention for at least the first six months of their life.

There are various legends about the Siamese cats. It is said that they were originally kept in the Royal palace as repositories for the souls of transmigrating Siamese Royalty. There is also a story about the kink in the tail (which, incidentally, is not liked at shows); a Princess of Siam hung her rings on her favourite cat's tail when she went bathing and the knot she tied so as not to lose them left the kink at the end. Whether there is any truth in these legends or not, they illustrate a long intimacy between these cats and humans, and nobody who has once been admitted into this intimacy can ever love any other animal quite so dearly.

Siamese cats are greedy, jealous – and destructive, since any piece of fine embroidery exists in their minds only as a suitable toy for their claws. But these faults fade beside their charms: their sense of humour, their fidelity, their dauntless courage, their playfulness, their conversational powers, their passionate interest in all that is going on around them, and the depth of affection which they are able to show in so many exquisite ways. They are clever with their paws, opening catches on doors and windows quite easily with their strong claws which, like the dog's, are never retracted.

Siamese must be kept happy and should never be confined in cages away from human contact, as they love people and are intensely curious. If they are left alone for long periods they will become bored and get into mischief, looking for anything they can destroy and tear to bits, knocking things down, and often howling at the top of their voices. So if you have to go out a lot, it is better to have two cats, or a cat and dog to keep each other company. They usually adopt one person in a household as their special friend, who may not be their actual owner.

For many years Blue and Chocolate Points were comparatively rare. Gradually the Blues increased and were recognized by the Governing Council of the Cat Fancy as a separate colour in 1936. The Chocolate Points gained recognition in 1951, and in 1961 the Lilac Points (called Frost Points in America) became the fourth colour variation. There are now Red Points, Tabby Points and Tortie Points as well, and these have been evolved by mating to the British cats. The standard has changed over the years; in the early days the face of the Siamese was much rounder than it is now, and some breeders are beginning to think that the breeding of cats with a very pointed face has gone too far and that the cats are losing their good chin shape. However, the American Standard for Siamese favours even narrower heads and longer, thinner bodies. Siamese are meant to be fairly heavy cats, especially the males; females should not be too small, or it will be difficult for them to produce healthy kittens and thin, scrawny kittens will be nervy and have little power of resistance when ill.

Siamese cats are very demanding, and although they should live as unrestricted a life as possible, care should be taken to treat them sensibly. Do not spoil them or they may rule your household. Never neglect any signs of illness, however, as Siamese are the most difficult invalids; they cannot bear to be ill and sometimes lack the will to live. If your pet is ill, never leave it to the care of other people, as knowing you are there will do much to ensure its recovery.

The Siamese is extremely intelligent and is usually very demanding (*right*). It is not the cat to choose if you have to be out of the house for long periods, as it is affectionate and loves to be in the company of humans.

The Tabby Point (*left*) is one of the very latest Siamese cats to receive recognition by The Governing Council of the Cat Fancy. It is a most attractive cat, with all the traditional qualities of the Siamese but it has, in addition, this outstanding colouring. The original Siamese Tabby Points were the results of a mis-alliance between a Seal Point Siamese female and a male of Tabby origin. Since the gene for tabby marking is dominant, the kittens born carried the pattern on the mask and points. The pale beauty of the coat highlighted by the pencilled tabby markings was enchanting and the variety was developed further. Tabby Point owners say their cats are gentler than most other Siamese varieties. In the United States of America the Tabby Point is known as the Lynx Point Siamese.

The dignity of this beautiful Siamese (*below left*) makes it easy to understand why the cat was revered in Ancient Egypt. It is probably from the name of the Cat Goddess Bast or Pasht that we get the diminutive 'Puss'. The Egyptians built a shrine to honour the cat-headed goddess on an island, probably to keep her from straying.

The coat pattern of the Abyssinian is unusual in that each hair has two or three separate bands of colour on it; the ground colour is a russet brown, and the bands are black or dark brown. However, there should be no banding on the inside of the forelegs and belly. This kitten (*right*) is a very good specimen, as he has the correct cream coloured chin, and virtually no tabby markings which many Abyssinians have on their legs and tails. The Abyssinian cat is said to resemble the cats worshipped by the Egyptians long ago and also the Caffre cat from which the early domestic cats were descended.

There are various legends about the Siamese cat. One tells of the Princess of Siam who long ago went to bathe in the river. Not knowing where to leave her valuable rings, she hooked them over the tail of her pet cat. All was well until the cat chased a butterfly and the rings fell off. The next time she tied a knot in the cat's tail so she would not lose the rings, and even today some Siamese have a kink in the tail as a result of the knot (*below*).

At birth Siamese kittens are pure white. When they are about a week old the points will begin to darken and by the time they are a month old they will be recognizable as Siamese. These kittens (*above and opposite*) have quite definitely established themselves as Seal Point and Chocolate Point Siamese.

The Red Point Siamese is a new breed to be accepted in Britain. When they conform to the standard they are very striking but there is difficulty still in eliminating the rings from their tails. These kittens (*below*) are only nine weeks old but already the tails bear the marks of their Red Tabby heritage.

The Blue Burmese (*below*) is not yet recognized by the Cat Fanciers' Association in America, although it is recognized in Britain. The body should be predominantly bluish-grey, with ears, mask and points shading to silver grey.

The Brown Burmese (*right*) differs from the Blue Burmese only in the colour of its coat, which should be a really dark shade of seal. The Burmese is the only natural breed of brown cat, the originals being the result of natural mating.

The Foreign White (*above*) is a recently recognized breed which is a Siamese cat with no points. A dominant gene produces the white coat, although it also carries the genetic information for coloured points.

The Seal Point on the right of this picture (*left*) shows clearly the requirements in a good specimen. The well-proportioned head, narrowing to a fine muzzle with width between the eyes, the mask, ears, feet and tail dense and clearly defined, the oval paws and extra long tail all gain points for the show cat. Siamese often have a tendency to squint. The eyes of this Blue Point are placed so that they appear to look permanently at the nose. This is considered a fault and would lose points.

The Siamese people often refer to the Siamese cat as the Chinese Cat. The first importations to appear in this country were the Seal Point, with the dark brown markings, which this young specimen (*right*) displays on his mask, ears and paws.

CATS ON SHOW

The best way to become known in the English Cat Fancy is by exhibiting your cats at the shows. In Britain they are held under the jurisdiction of the Governing Council of the Cat Fancy, which issues licences to clubs to hold shows, providing they are affiliated to the Governing Council and are prepared to obey rules laid down by this body. There are three types of cat show: Exemption, Sanction and Championship.

Exemption shows are very good to attend and exhibit at if you are a beginner as, although the general rules are greatly relaxed, professional judges will be officiating and you can get from them a valuable assessment of your cat, kitten or neuter, and of your non-pedigree cats as well. You can compare your exhibits with others, join the Club and get to know other owners who will soon help you with plenty of advice.

Sanction shows are rehearsals for shows with Championship status, so everything must be carried out as at a Championship show. At a Championship show official judges are empowered to award or withhold championship certificates, and your cat will need three, awarded by different judges of the breed at three different shows in order to become a champion.

If you mean to show your cat, it is essential that he should be used to being handled. Most cats love shows, but occasionally you get a cat who appears to suffer from claustrophobia, refuses point blank to be removed from his pen and flies at the unlucky judge or steward who attempts to handle him. If your cat is like this, accept it. Do not show him again or he will get a reputation for bad temper that he probably does not deserve. It is against the rules to give a cat sedatives, so accept the situation to save yourself and others real trouble. Some people think that a stud cat will not be used if he does not become a champion, or that kittens will not be bought if the queen is not a champion. This is a fallacy, for it is known that cats attaining this status are not always the best breeders. Likewise, many un-shown cats breed winning kittens, provided they are well bred themselves.

A pedigree cat is one whose ancestors are known for at least three or four generations. To enter a show licensed by the GCCF a cat or kitten must be registered, and once a cat is registered it must not be entered in an unlicensed show without permission from the Council. Household cats need not be registered and can be entered in the special classes provided for them. Registered neuters can also compete for Premier certificates at Championship shows but only cats can compete for challenge certificates. Single kittens may not be exhibited until they are at least three months old, except at a few summer shows, where they may be accepted at eight weeks. Single Siamese and Burmese kittens are not accepted under the age of four months. Some shows have litter classes for three or more kittens from the same litter between the ages of ten and twelve weeks. A kitten becomes a cat at nine months.

Never attempt to show a cat that is out of condition or not well groomed. Long-hairs need a great deal of preparation. Brush and comb your cat or kitten every day so that only the finishing touches are needed on show day. Long-haired Blacks, Reds and Brown Tabbies need to be cleaned with cotton wool pads soaked in eau-de-cologne. Points are lost for a Long-haired or Short-haired White if it has a stained yellow tail. These cats need to be powdered carefully, and sometimes bathed before a show. Before undertaking this, get advice from people who deal with these particular breeds. Powder must not be left in a cat's coat for judging, and it is against the rules to brush it out in the hall on the morning of the show. Short-haired cats need grooming too, and Siamese benefit from an overnight bran bath. Daily hand grooming cannot be bettered for all Short-haired breeds, as their coats lie flat, whereas the Long-hairs' coats are brushed upwards towards the head and should never be smoothed down flat.

Continental cat shows have been held in various parts of the Continent and Scandinavia since 1924, and since 1950 the number of shows has greatly increased. Their method differs from the British and American style in many ways. Cat shows in Australia and New Zealand are run on the same principle as those in Britain, but one-day shows are more popular. The American Cat Fancy is much larger than the British and there are several governing bodies in the various States and many clubs catering for all breeds.

A feature of the Continental and Scandinavian shows is the two or three day 'exposition'. Members only exhibit, no entry fees are paid and there is no prize money. All exhibits receive a certificate signed by the judge and at the end of the last day prizes are presented, some very beautiful and valuable. These are donated by Patrons, Officers, Committee members and friends. Pens are decorated before the show opens and make a colourful display which the public appreciate and enjoy.

The White Long-hair *(right)* wins great admiration at cat shows. Also known as the White Persian, this breed can have blue, green, orange or yellow eyes and some have odd eyes. If you want to show your cat, however, there are class numbers only for Blue, Orange or Odd-eyed Whites.

The Red Colourpoint kitten (*left*) shows clearly the combination of the popular Siamese colouring with the Persian type. Colourpoints are now being bred in all the various Siamese colourings. In America they are known as Himalayan cats, and the Red Colourpoint is recognized by the American Cat Fancy, though not by the British organization.

For show purposes the background colour of the Red Tabby, one of the most attractive Short-hairs, should be a really rich red, while the markings must be a distinctly darker shade. This kitten (*below left*) is well marked and the coat will darken as it grows older.

The Blue Long-hair (*above right*) is often regarded as the cat most likely to succeed in the show ring. Because of the quality of the coat it is a breed often used to improve the standard of other Long-haired varieties. The body type is typical of the Long-hairs, big but not ungainly, with round and broad head, tiny, well-tufted ears showing a good width between them. The eyes should be large and round, orange or copper red in colour. The colour of the coat ranges from the palest lavender to deep sapphire. It is important for the show cats that the colour is uniform throughout. It can be light, medium or dark blue but there must be no patches of white hairs in the coat. The frill must be the same colour as the fur on the other parts of the body; a pale frill is considered a fault.

The Brown Tabby Long-hair (*right*) is perhaps the most natural looking of all the more highly bred cats. However, it is a breed that has lost its popularity and as a result there are very few breeders. One of the faults, and a persistent one, is the white chin. It is taking breeders a long time to eradicate it from the Brown Tabby.

The Cream Long-hair (*above*) has a grin that would be the envy of the Cheshire Cat! The colour of this breed should, ideally, be true throughout the coat, with each hair unshaded from the root to the tip. Breeders try to produce a cool colour, as there is a tendency for the shade to become more of a warm apricot than a cool cream.

It is said that the Russian Blue, once called the Archangel Blue (*left*), used to be the pets of the Tsars of Russia, but others deny there is a trace of Russian in them. The Russian Blue is longer in the leg than the British cat, and finer boned.

The Tabby Point Siamese are real show stoppers as they have pale bodies with tabby points, fine, well ringed tails with solid black tips, black stockings up the backs of the hind legs and wide ears with black 'thumb marks' at the back. This cat (*right*) is in first class condition and his bright eyes and alert appearance give every indication of his energy and good health.

The Blue Cream Long-hair (*above*) is sometimes called the Blue Tortoise-shell but this name is more applicable to the Blue Creams of the United States of America, where the colours may be in solid patches. As in all long-haired cats, the coat must be long and flowing, and in Britain and on the Continent the colours must be pastel shades of blue and cream, softly intermingled to give the hazy appearance of watered silk. The eyes should be deep orange or copper-coloured. Like the Blue Cream Short-haired cats, these Long-hairs are not easily obtained because of the difficulties in breeding them. Blue Cream kittens are enchanting in their curiosity and sense of fun, and they are bold and intelligent. A fully grown Blue Cream makes a charming companion, placid and delightful in every way.

This trio of Blue Burmese kittens (*left*) have found themselves something to keep them amused – and out of other mischief! This breed is a fairly recent development from the Brown Burmese, and has been recognized by the British Cat Fancy since 1960.

Perhaps the reason for the Cream Short-hair (*right*) being so rare at shows is that its colour must be a rich cream with no signs of white and it must be free from bars. Quite often very young kittens have perfect colouring, only to develop bars on the legs and rings on the tail as they grow.

The even patching of the Tortoiseshell and White cat is very difficult to achieve. Although this cat (*left*) is not a perfect show specimen, it is in its favour that the patches are clearly defined.

The blueness of the coat of the British Blue (*right*) is most attractive when it is a medium shade, and it is important that the coat should be really short. This breed has been described by some people as the aristocrat of British Short-hairs.

When the Abyssinians were first recognized, kittens of a copper red colour appeared from time to time and breeders were barred from showing them because this colour did not fit the breed. Eventually, however, they were recognized as a separate variety and today the Red Abyssinian (*left*), known as the Sorrel in the United States, is a breed in its own right.

Cats with long hair have existed in Persia for many centuries but until the last century all cats in the Western Hemisphere had short, thick coats. Breeders interested in introducing a longer-coated cat imported some of these cats from Persia. First they were taken to France, then later they came to England to improve the length of hair in the English cats. At the beginning this new breed was known as Angora but at a later date it was changed to Persian. Now they are just called Long-hairs. This little kitten (*below left*) has yet to grow his magnificent coat and the flowing ruff which is typical of these cats.

The Red Long-hair (*above right*) is rare, possibly because judicious breeding to Blue and Black, which necessitates long-term planning in order to be successful, has been avoided in the past. It is very difficult to breed a cat free from tabby markings, and it is unfortunate that this most striking, copper-eyed variety is so seldom seen on the show bench.

Colour and marking of the Manx cat (*above far right*) are a secondary consideration at shows. It is the essential characteristics of the breed which are important to the judges. These are taillessness, height of hindquarters, shortness of back and depth of flank. It is a combination of these features which give this cat its rabbity gait. The double coat is also like that of a rabbit. The undercoat is very thick and soft and there is another thick coat of long hairs as well.

The colour of the Cameo cat, a combination of cream and red, has been developed over a period of twenty years in America, where they are recognized as a breed. There are four shades of this breed, and the sparkling Tabby Cameo (*right*) shows clearly the beautiful markings essential to this variety.

THE BIG CATS

Most of the Big Cats live in Asia and are classed with the Domestic Cats in a group called Felidae. The best known are the Lion, Leopard, Tiger, Puma, Cheetah, Jaguar and Ocelot; specimens of these breeds can be seen in the big zoos at home and abroad and in the wildlife reservations which various governments have set up to preserve them. An exception is the Snow Leopard, which is found in Tibet. The Puma is native to both North and South America, and is also called the Mountain Lion. The Cheetah, said to be the fastest animal in the world, can be domesticated but has never been known to breed in captivity.

The Lynx is a smaller wild cat and is found in many places. The African Lynx has large ears with tufts of hair at the tips; the coat colour is pale, rusty red to grey. It is said that the Abyssinian cat is descended from the African Lynx and the tufted ears, the coat colour and the ability to swim support this theory. On the other hand, the Abyssinian cat is often called the Little Lion because of its resemblance to the lioness in colour, expression and coat pattern. The Tabby cat has been likened to the Tiger and the Leopard to the Indian desert cat, which has a spotted yellow coat and is probably one of the ancestors of our Spotted domestic cat. Another close relative to domestic cats could be the African Kaffir cat which is yellow in colour and known to mate with domestics. It is interesting to note that the Big Cats are short-haired; the exceptions are the Lion, with his mane of long hair, and the Pallas Cat which has a long coat and bushy tail.

We cannot be absolutely certain when cats came to Britain, but it is likely that they were brought by the Romans, who regarded them as prized possessions. It is probable the European wild cat, Felis Sylvestris, was already established by then. Today the Scottish Wild Cat, Felis Sylvestris Grampia, is on the increase in Scotland. They are quite untamable; even kittens found abandoned are spitting bundles of fury. A few wild cats are known to have mated with domestic cats, probably the wilder type found on isolated farms. The Scottish Wild Cats are larger than domestic ones; they have larger, flatter heads and their ears often turn downwards, probably as a natural protection.

Domestic cats with folded ears have appeared during the last ten years on a farm in Scotland; these are a mutation and may be the result of matings between a wild cat and a feral farm cat. The litters are usually mixed, some having ordinary ears. It is claimed that the folded-ear cats are sometimes deaf and the majority of breeders consider them abnormal. A few interested people would like them recognized as a new breed but it is unlikely that the Governing Council of the Cat Fancy will agree to do so.

During the last war many cats fled from bombed areas and became wild, living on bomb sites and in wooded areas, fending for themselves. Many were rescued and became tame again, some had to be trapped and destroyed, and many others died from exposure and neglect. There are stories of these poor cats who crawled into people's outhouses to die, having the instinct to get among humans again.

Cats have had a chequered existence, loved by some, hated by others. Today many have loving owners and good homes but many more are thrown out to roam the streets, all too often meeting a fate worse than death in a laboratory. Cats are beautiful and clever animals but they are independent and do not appeal to the people who prefer the utter devotion of a dog. Cats have a sense of direction and can find their way back to their homes and owners, covering many miles; although they may appear aloof, they can be very devoted.

Most of the Big Cats live in warm climates. One of the few exceptions is the Snow Leopard *(left)*, which is found on the snowy heights of Tibet where it is protected by an ample furry coat. Unfortunately the lovely coat has been coveted by fashion-conscious ladies and the number of Snow Leopards has become dangerously depleted.

Lions are the largest, heaviest and most powerful of all the cat family, but they can be quite easily frightened. The male differs greatly in appearance from other cats, having long hair on his head and shoulders, which is the mane, and a tuft of hair on the end of his tail. The female *(right)* does not have any of these adornments and looks more like the domestic cat.

'One needs to watch the cat at work to see the tiger in the hearth.' So goes the old saying, but when you are sitting with puss curled up on your knee it is difficult to imagine that he is alert to every movement. When the moment is right, quick as a flash every muscle will spring into action and a lightning paw will shoot out with deadly aim on some unsuspecting prey (*below*).

The Wild Cat (*below right*) was common in Britain until the early nineteenth century. When firearms were introduced and forests were cleared the Wild Cat was brought almost to extinction, except in Scotland where it is now on the increase. Although the Wild Cat resembles the domesticated Tabby, it is more heavily built. The head is broad and square with abundant whiskers, the fur is thicker than that of the domestic Tabby and the tail ends with a blunt tip, unlike that of the domestic cat which

tapers to a point. The Wild Cat lives in the thickly wooded areas in the Highlands where it can find protection among the rocks and trees. Since it has increased in numbers it has begun to move further south.

The teeth of all cats, wild or domesticated, are developed to give a firm hold on struggling prey. They are sharpened into scissor-like blades which can pare meat from a bone.

Cat lived on earth many millions of years before Man. It is possible to confirm this fact from the skeletal remains of the extinct Sabre-toothed Tiger of prehistoric times. A skull of one of these animals was found in a cave in Brazil, similar to the cat of today in its teeth formation. There are six teeth at the top front, and these are very small and simple; six teeth grow in the lower jaw and they are even smaller. The next tooth on either side in each jaw is the large, strong, conical

tooth, which is curved and sharply pointed. The small size of the front teeth in contrast makes the larger teeth look quite fearsome.

The Leopard (*right*) is one of the smaller of the Big Cats, similar to the Jaguar. The ground colour of its coat is usually a dark shade of yellow and this is marked by black spots mainly arranged in rosettes, the centres being a darker shade than the general ground colour. Leopards live in a variety of habitats, from jungle to grassland and from semi-desert to snow-covered highlands. They are found throughout Africa and much of Asia.

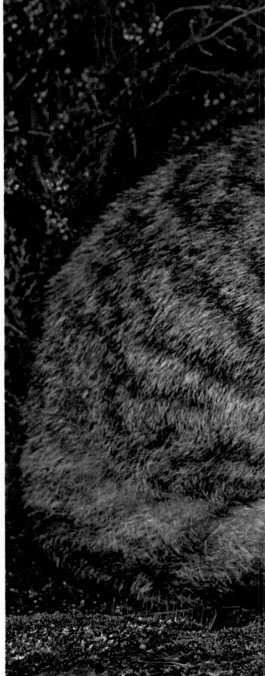

84

When lion cubs are born they are fully furred and have grey spots with rosettes which gradually fade as they grow older (*above*). They do not have full sight until they are about two weeks old, and at three weeks the teeth start to appear. As soon as the cubs are able to leave the den, they go back to their mother's pride. A pride varies in size from three of four up to thirty and, although not strictly a family group, the nucleus is formed of the leader, or king, several lionesses and their young. When the cubs are six months old they will join in the hunt. The mother will have to teach them how to stalk and kill their prey, how to follow the pride and generally fend for themselves. They become independent when they are one and a half to two years old and reach maturity at three to four years old.

The cats who live in a colony in the Forum in Rome live really as wild cats, but their well-being lacks nothing, as you can see by the appearance of this cat lying in the shade of a tomb (*left*). He is obviously happy, relaxed and well fed. Cats were introduced to Rome, it is supposed, by the Egyptians. It is also reasonable to suppose that the cat was brought to Britain by the Romans. The evidence to support this lies in the fact that clear imprints of cats' paws have been found in tiles in Roman villas built during the first centuries of the Christian era.

All cats, with the exception of the Lion and the Tiger, which are the largest and heaviest of the family, are expert climbers. This Jungle Cat (*above*) has found himself a place in the branches where his camouflage is almost perfect, and with the sun dappling his coat, he would be very difficult to see. Most of the Big Cats are rarely seen and unless they are in a tight spot, or are defending their young, they seldom attack humans.

The Tiger (*right*) is the largest of the cats but is slimmer and narrower in the body than the Lion. The ground colour of the Tiger's coat is reddish fawn, broken at intervals by dark vertical stripes. This colouring provides a natural camouflage against the patterns of light and shade in the natural surroundings.

The Ocelot (*above*), one of the small wild cats of America, is becoming increasingly popular as a pet. They are easily tamed and make intelligent, playful and absorbing companions. As can be seen, they are extremely decorative, even if rather more alarming at first sight than the domestic cat.

At birth the coat of the Cheetah kittens (*above right*) is a blue-grey colour on the back and the rest is brown with dark spots. Gradually, the ground colour lightens until, like their mother, they will be a reddish yellow broken by spots of solid black. The face is marked with striking 'tear stripes' running from the eyes to the end of the nose.

The young, fierce-looking lioness (*right*) has almost reached maturity. When she is fully grown she will stand about 30 in at the shoulder and weigh up to 400 lb. The jaws and forelegs are enormously powerful and one swift blow from her paw can break the neck of a zebra or antelope.

CATS ON THEIR OWN

Almost everyone who has a pet will need to make use of a boarding kennels at holiday time or in cases of special emergency. If you are concerned about your cat, you will want to look at all the available accommodation in your district and, even if you are recommended to a place, do not arrange to take your pet there until you have first inspected it. When you find a place you like and that your cat subsequently also likes, stick to it so that your cat will become familiar with the surroundings and the people in charge.

If you have a cat that is very settled in its habits, you may have a friend who will go in twice a day to feed it and change its tray. Never leave it to fend for itself and never leave it behind unprotected if you move house or leave the district. If you cannot take the cat and are unable to find it a suitable home, it is better to have it painlessly put to sleep. If, however, you can find the cat a home, make sure it is suitable. People often say they will take a cat but if it does not settle down quickly or seem to be fond of them, they may become impatient with it and neglect it. Some cats are undoubtedly unhappy at leaving their familiar home. They may be scared of another cat, dog or child in the new place, be afraid to move about much and so may become dirty. Many people will not have it on their conscience that they had a healthy animal put to sleep, but they do not stop to consider that by giving it away they may be condemning it to a worse fate.

Cats are often quite happy the first week they are away, for the change of scene and people will interest them. If they are going to become mopy it usually shows itself in the second week. This is the time that they are most likely to pick up any infection, so the place where you leave your cat should have runs divided from one another by a solid partition as well as wire netting. This prevents direct contact with a sneezing cat, should there be one there. In the best type of boarding kennels the houses will not be under one roof. The house should have a sleeping compartment, a shelf under a window and a door for the cat to get in and out at will. Heating should be available for cold nights and winter boarding.

A deep sanitary tray should be provided. If possible runs should be of concrete with a pot of grass for the cat. Make sure fastenings on doors and windows are safe, for many a cat has escaped from a run-down place. Let your cat have its own blanket, favourite toy and, if there is room, its box or basket. On the whole cats and kittens are happy in catteries and eat well, and they soon know if they are well looked after. Do not attempt to take your cat if it is not well, as it is not fair on the owners nor on the other cats. Most kennel owners require a veterinary certificate to say that your pet has been inoculated against feline enteritis. Give the cattery owner a diet sheet and tell him if your cat has any peculiar habits. Be sure your cat has clean ears and a coat free from fleas or other pests. Leave your address and be sure to say goodbye to your pet and assure him that you will soon be back, as cats are hypersensitive and really do understand what is going on around them.

However much you love your cat, do not go without a holiday because you think its way of life must not be disturbed. Some people put animals into the same category as humans, which is wrong. They cannot think as we do, but if it really makes you unhappy to go away without your pet, arrange a holiday in a caravan or country cottage.

People who run good kennels do make an income, but the work is hard and never finished. One has to be on hand all the time and it is too much work for one person, as you will find that to board only half a dozen cats will take up a great deal of time. Cleaning houses, cooking and preparing food, washing dishes and blankets, putting down fresh water and changing sanitary trays at least twice a day all makes a lot of work. So do not undertake this way of making money unless you are dedicated to cats' welfare.

Cruelty to animals is a terrible thing. It is possible that cruelty to cats is more evident than to any other animal, although all suffer in their various ways. There are now numerous welfare societies for the protection of cats, though cats nowadays are often treated as badly as they were a hundred years ago. People still have to be urged not to desert cats when they move house or go on holiday, not to let children torment them, and not to ill-treat or starve them. Cats nowadays face even greater hazards from the cat stealers who pick up healthy cats and sell them to dealers who, in turn, hand them over to laboratories for experimental purposes.

Dogs are protected by law in a way that does not apply to cats; a stray dog or one that is run over in the road must be taken to a police station for a report to be made, but not so a cat. It is all the more important, therefore, for us to take very great care of our cats.

Many cats become strays when their owners move house or go away on holiday, which is a deplorable way of treating any pet. This little kitten (*right*) is obviously well cared for. He is lively and ready for a romp just as soon as the invitation of that look is accepted.

The two Tortoiseshell cats (*above*) are quite devoted and, though they may fight occasionally, on the whole there is nothing they will not do for each other. Cats are capable of great affection and if two from the same litter have the good fortune to live their lives together they will probably be inseparable.

The cat has a knack for finding surroundings complimentary to its own beauty. It can often be found in the garden among the brightest flowers and it seems to choose the colours which go best with its own coat colour. The colour of this orange and white Bi-coloured cat (*left*) is cleverly accentuated by the gold of the crocuses.

The aloof yet endearing look on the face of this Tabby (*right*) is baffling. He appears relaxed, yet at any moment he could give you an intimidating stare, or a swipe with a powerful paw. The independence and inscrutability of cats is one of their main attractions.

It is a mistaken idea to suppose that a cat will make a better mouser if it is kept hungry. Cats are natural predators (*left*) and will have more vitality and stamina to do the job if they are fed regularly. Often the cat will earn the dislike of bird lovers when it kills small birds but the percentage of birds killed and eaten is lower than that of rodents and insects. Cats are classed as wild animals and the owner of a cat cannot be held responsible for the misdeeds of his pet.

Most household pets conform to no particular standards for cats. Like this one (*right*), they are the mongrel offspring of centuries of free mating. Cats are notoriously promiscuous but this does not make them less charming and lovable, for they possess a beauty all their own.

In busy Baghdad where the Arabs crowded the famous silk bazaar, cats were to be seen all around. The name of the bazaar was Attabiah, after the watered silk which was made there. Since the pattern of the cats resembled the effect of the silk, the name 'tabby' was attached to these brindled cats (*below right*).

It isn't really quite the thing to do, to hide in the skin of your distant relative. This little kitten (*below far right*) only knows that it is soft and comfortable, and that this tiger skin definitely matches his colouring.